W9-DIB-639

A Look At...

Voyages of Exploration

WORLD BOOK

a Scott Fetzer company
Chicago
www.worldbookonline.com

Staff:

Executive Committee

President
Donald D. Keller

Vice President and Editor
in Chief
Paul A. Kobasa

Vice President, Marketing/
Digital Products
Sean Klunder

Vice President,
International
Richard Flower

Director, Human Resources
Bev Ecker

Editorial

Associate Director,
Supplementary Publications
Scott Thomas

Associate Manager,
Supplementary Publications
Cassie Mayer

Researcher,
Supplementary Publications
Annie Brodsky

Manager, Indexing Services
David Pofelski

Manager, Contracts & Compliance
(Rights & Permissions)
Loranne K. Shields

Editorial Administration

Director, Systems and Projects
Tony Tills

Senior Manager, Publishing
Operations
Timothy Falk

Associate Manager,
Publishing Operations
Audrey Casey

Graphics and Design

Manager
Tom Evans

Manager, Cartographic Services
Wayne K. Pichler

Senior Cartographer
John Rejba

Book Design by
Matt Carrington

Senior Designer
Isaiah Sheppard

Contributing Designer
Lucy Lesiak

Photo Editor
Kathy Creech

Contributing Photo Editor
Clover Morell

Production

Director, Manufacturing and Pre-Press
Carma Fazio

Manufacturing Manager
Steven K. Hueppchen

Production/
Technology Manager
Anne Fritzinger

Proofreader
Emilie Schrage

World Book, Inc.
233 N. Michigan Avenue
Chicago, IL 60601

For information about other World Book publications, visit our website at http://www.worldbookonline.com or call **1-800-WORLDBK (967-5325).**
For information about sales to schools and libraries, call **1-800-975-3250 (United States)**, or **1-800-837-5365 (Canada).**

Library of Congress Cataloging-in-Publication Data
Voyages of exploration
    p. cm. -- (A look at ...)
  Includes index.
  Summary: "An introduction to the early centuries of exploration, including information about explorers, what they discovered, and the significance of those discoveries. Features include fact boxes, maps, photographs, drawings, a timeline, a glossary, and a list of recommended books and websites."--Provided by publisher.
  ISBN 978-0-7166-1793-8
  1. Discoveries in geography--Juvenile literature.
2. Explorers--Juvenile literature. I. World Book, Inc.
G175.V69 2011
910.9--dc22

                        2011005431

A Look At ...
Set ISBN 978-0-7166-1786-0

Printed in China by Shenzhen Donnelley Printing Co., Ltd.
Guangdong Province
1st printing July 2011

Picture Acknowledgments:

The publishers gratefully acknowledge the following sources for photography. All illustrations and maps were prepared by WORLD BOOK unless otherwise noted.

Front Cover: Shutterstock

Art Resource 43; BrazilPhotos/Alamy Images 41; Classic Image/Alamy Images 28, 53; Mary Evans Picture Library/Alamy Images 8, 54, 58; INTERFOTO/Alamy Images 8, 18, 24; Lou Linwei/Alamy Images 11; North Wind Pictures/Alamy Images 11, 12, 13, 27, 32, 36, 40, 46, 48, 50, 53; PARIS PIERCE/Alamy Images 52; Penny Tweedie, Alamy Images 54; Photos 12/Alamy Images 19; Robert Harding Picture Library/Alamy Images 9; SCPhotos/Alamy Images 6; The Art Gallery Collection/Alamy Images 10, 30, 31, 34; The National Trust Photolibrary/Alamy Images; Bridgeman Art Library 40; Dreamstime 33, 57; Bridgeman Art Library/Getty Images 5, 20, 26; ChinaFotoPress/Getty Images 6; DEA/G. DAGLI ORTI/Getty Images 29; Hulton Archive/Getty Images 16, 34, 61; Karen Bleier, AFP/Getty Images 41; MPI/Getty Images 37; Robert F. Sisson, National Geographic/Getty Images 45; SSPL/Getty Images 59; Stock Montage/Getty Images 39; Time Life Pictures/Getty Image 17; Enrique Shore, Reuters/Landov 20; Library of Congress 14; Library Of Congress Geography and Map Division 15, 25; National Library of Australia 18; North Wind Pictures 49; Shutterstock 12, 14, 18, 22, 31, 42, 46, 47, 56; The Art Archive/SuperStock 38, 60

CONTENTS

There is a glossary on page 62. Terms defined in the glossary are in type that looks like this on their first appearance on any spread (two facing pages).

Introducing Voyages of Exploration

People have always wondered what lies beyond the horizon. Over time, people have made voyages to nearly all regions of the world.

Human beings possess a strong sense of curiosity. They have never been satisfied to stay put for long. Scientists who study people of long ago think that some of our human ancestors journeyed out of their homeplaces in Africa to other continents nearly 2 million years ago.

The first human migrants (travelers) almost certainly walked. In time, however, people learned to domesticate animals that could be ridden and build boats to travel by water.

People gain knowledge about how to make or do something by trial and error. When they find something that works, they pass it on to other people. Such useful knowledge is called technology.

As the centuries passed, people developed better technology for building ships. This book is about the Age of Exploration, a period of discovery that began among Europeans around A.D. 1400. However, many earlier explorers made voyages of discovery.

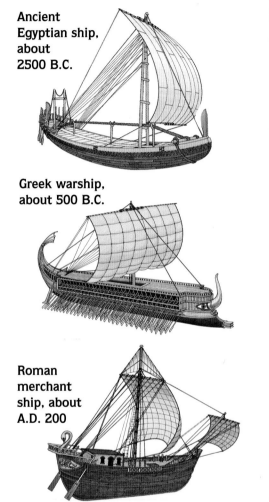

Ancient Egyptian ship, about 2500 B.C.

Greek warship, about 500 B.C.

Roman merchant ship, about A.D. 200

Voyages in Greek and Roman times

The ancient Egyptians, Greeks, and Romans greatly improved technologies for building ships. They designed cargo ships to carry goods in trade. They also designed warships to defend their shores or to take over other lands by sea.

The Dark Ages in Europe

Between the A.D. 100's and 200's, half of Europe, much of the Middle East, and the north coast of Africa were governed by the **Roman Empire** from its capital, ancient Rome. In Europe, the period after the fall of the Roman Empire in the late A.D. 400's is sometimes referred to as "the Dark Ages." During this period, life became so difficult that most people worked the land and stayed close to home. However, at about the same time, Islamic societies in North Africa and the Middle East flourished. An Islamic society is primarily made up of **Muslims,** people of the Islamic faith. This society continued to explore and discover.

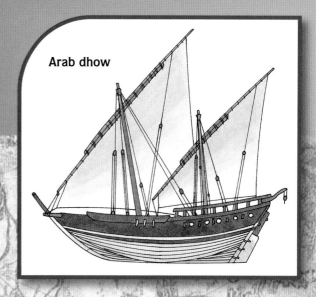

Arab dhow

Islamic explorers

One of the most famous and successful Islamic explorers was Ibn Battuta *(IHB uhn bat TOO tah)*, who lived during the 1300's. Battuta, an Arab, was born in what is now Morocco in North Africa.

Ibn Battuta visited Egypt, Ethiopia, Syria, Asia Minor (now part of Turkey), Persia (now parts of Iraq, Iran, and Afghanistan), India, Indonesia, and China. He recorded his travels in a book called *Rihla (Journey).* Ibn Battuta traveled both by land and sea. On the sea, he probably traveled in an Arab boat called a *dhow (DOW).*

A map made in Venice in about 1540 has Europe at the center of the world. Although the Age of Discovery increased European knowledge of the world, Europeans saw themselves as the world's masters.

About 100 years after Ibn Battuta made his voyages of discovery, a Chinese explorer sailed from China to the west, reaching as far as the Cape of Good Hope in South Africa.

Chinese explorers

In the early 1400's, the Chinese **emperor** (powerful ruler) wanted to make contact with other countries in Asia and the Middle East. He had workers build a huge **fleet** (group of warships) and selected a famous soldier named Zheng He *(juhng huh)* to lead it.

Historians believe that Zheng He's fleet included about 300 ships and 30,000 sailors. Among the ships were treasure junks—massive wooden sailing ships on which valuable cargo was stored. (*Junk* is the Chinese word for ship.) Some scholars think that a Chinese treasure junk may have been 10 times the size of a European ship of the time. Most agree that it is the largest wooden ship ever launched.

The Chinese still use junks to carry goods and passengers along coasts and on rivers.

A replica of Zheng He's treasure junk shows what the massive ship may have looked like.

Voyages westward

In 1405, Zheng He guided his great fleet out of the mouth of China's Yangtze *(yahng dzuh)* River onto the open sea. The ships traveled all the way to India, stopping at many points along the way.

Between 1407 and 1433, Zheng He made six more voyages. He explored what are now the countries of Vietnam, Indonesia, Malaysia, Sri Lanka, India, and Iran, and on to the Arabian peninsula and the east coast of Africa.

As Zheng He made his voyages, most Europeans remained unaware of the world beyond Europe. That would soon change. The Age of Exploration was about to begin.

The Age of Exploration refers to the exciting period between the 1400's and the 1700's. During this time, most voyages of discovery were sponsored by European rulers or companies. Below is a list of important events in the European Age of Exploration.

Date	Event
1487	Bartholomeu Dias (Portugal) rounds the southern tip of Africa and sails into the Indian Ocean.
1492	Christopher Columbus (Spain) lands on an island in the West Indies.
1497	Vasco da Gama (Portugal) sails around Africa and across the Indian Ocean to India.
1498	Columbus sights the northern coast of South America and realizes that it is a continent.
1500	Pedro Cabral (Portugal) sights Brazil and names it.
1513	Vasco de Balboa (Spain) becomes the first European to see the Pacific Ocean.
1519–1522	Magellan and del Cano (Spain) make the first sea voyage around the world.
1521	Hernán Cortés (Spain) conquers Mexico.
1532	Francisco Pizarro (Spain) conquers Peru.
1539–1542	De Soto and Coronado (Spain) separately explore lands in what is now the southern United States.
1557	Portugal starts the colony of Macau on the coast of China.
1607	The English found Jamestown, their first permanent settlement in North America.
1608	Samuel de Champlain (France) founds Quebec and starts the colony of New France in North America.
1609–1611	Henry Hudson (Netherlands) explores the Hudson River and Hudson Bay in North America.
1642	Abel Tasman (Netherlands) sights the Australian island of Tasmania and New Zealand.
1730's	John Harrison (United Kingdom) invents the chronometer, a tool that greatly improved **navigation.**
1741	Vitus Bering (Russia) sights Alaska.
1778	Captain James Cook (United Kingdom) lands on the Hawaiian Islands.

The Vikings

Before the Age of Exploration began, the Vikings explored new lands in the North Atlantic Ocean. Few other Europeans of that time traveled very far from home.

The Vikings lived in what is now Scandinavia. (Scandinavia includes the modern countries of Denmark, Norway, and Sweden.) The Vikings were also known as the Norsemen.

The Vikings farmed and raised their own food. They also built ships for fishing and became skilled handlers of boats and ships at sea. In the late A.D. 700's, life among the Vikings became harder. The population was growing, and good farmland was running out. For these reasons, Viking warriors began making voyages by sea and raiding other areas of Europe, such as England, Ireland, and northern France.

The Vikings had the best ship technology in Europe. Viking ship designers added a keel (strong rib at the bottom of a boat extending down its length) to their long boats, which made the ships faster and easier to steer. Viking seafarers also learned how to figure out **latitude** (how far north or south one is) by recording the position of the sun at midday for each week of the year.

The Vikings are best known for their long ships. They sailed these swift, narrow vessels across the unknown waters of the Atlantic Ocean to North America.

Vikings stop on the shores of Scotland to prepare for their voyage to Greenland.

This wood engraving depicts Viking ships arriving at the west coast of Greenland in the 1000's.

The Vikings explore and discover

Between the A.D. 700's and 1000's, Viking sailors and warriors went on longer voyages in their long boats. They traveled beyond the world then known by Europeans.

One group of Vikings traveled west from Norway. Around 870, they discovered the island of Iceland, about 650 miles (1,050 kilometers) west of Norway. Many Vikings soon settled there.

Around 982, a Viking named Erik the Red sailed with his family from Iceland to Greenland, about 200 miles (320 kilometers) to the west. Greenland, the world's largest island, lies just off the coast of North America.

About 1000, Leif Eriksson, a son of Erik the Red, led an **expedition** (voyage of exploration) westward from Greenland and landed somewhere along the east coast of North America. They spent the winter there. Leif called the area Vinland, or Wineland, because they made wine from grapes they found there.

Historians do not know for sure where Vinland was. Many believe that it was the island of Newfoundland, which today is part of Canada. The Vinland colony lasted only a short time. It marked the first time that Europeans had made contact with the Americas. Christopher Columbus would "discover" America nearly 500 years later.

Leif Eriksson led what is believed to have been the first voyage to the mainland of North America in about A.D. 1000.

Vikings in Minnesota?

In 1898, a farmer named Olaf Ohman claimed that he found an ancient stone with writing on his farm near Kensington, Minnesota. The writing was in the form of runes—characters from an alphabet that the Vikings used. When translated, the writing contained a message supposedly written in 1362. The stone and its writing suggested that the Vikings had reached the middle of the North American continent nearly 700 years ago. Many—but not all—scholars have said the stone is a fake. We may never know the truth about the so-called Kensington rune stone.

The Vikings sailed from Scandinavia in three main directions from the A.D. 700's to the 1000's.

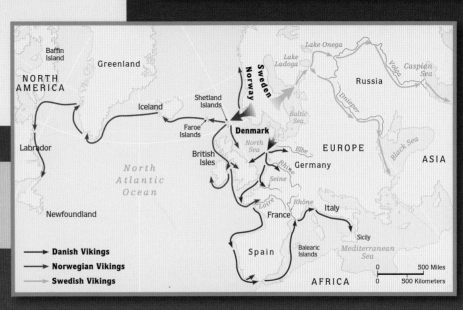

Marco Polo

In the 1200's, an adventurous Italian merchant named Marco Polo traveled to China. After he returned to Italy years later, Polo wrote a book about his experiences in China.

Long ago, travel was slow and difficult, especially by land. There were few roads. People walked, rode horseback, or rode in wagons pulled by horses or oxen.

Despite these hardships, some traders managed to carry goods long distances. Through such trade, people in Europe became aware of riches from far-distant places. One such place was China. Silk, porcelain, and other fine goods arrived in Europe from China through trading. However, people in Europe knew almost nothing about China.

In the 1200's, Italians were the most successful merchants and traders. One such wealthy trader was Nicolò Polo. In the 1260's, Nicolò Polo and his brother Maffeo led a trading **expedition** to China. They returned to Italy in 1269.

To China again

In 1271, the Polo brothers again departed for China. This time, they took Nicolò's 17-year-old son, Marco, with them. The Polos traveled partly by sea and partly by land to the East. The journey took three years. During their first visit to China, Nicolò and Maffeo Polo had become known to Kublai Khan, China's ruler. They continued to enjoy his favor on the second trip. The Polos stayed in China for about 17 years. During this time, Kublai Khan sent Marco Polo on many official missions throughout China.

Marco Polo became famous for his journeys in central Asia and China.

Approximate **routes** (paths) to and from Asia taken by Marco Polo and his family in the 1200's.

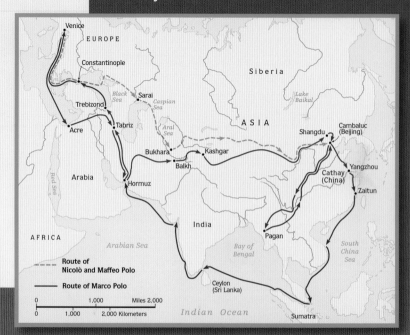

Marco Polo writes a book

After the Polos returned to Venice from China in 1295, Marco wrote a book describing his travels. The book, called *Description of the World,* was handwritten and then copied many times, because the printing press was not yet known in Europe. Later, the book became known as *The Travels of Marco Polo.*

Europeans were eager to hear about the strange, distant land of China. Marco Polo described great cities connected by canals (human-made waterways) and the fine palaces of Kublai Khan. He also described paper money and coal used as fuel. These items were unknown among Europeans of Polo's time. Marco Polo's writings spread through Europe and awakened curiosity among Europeans about far-distant lands.

The Polos were among the first Europeans to experience Chinese architecture and culture.

Marco Polo rides in one of Kublai Khan's elephant cars during his stay in China in the 1200's.

Desire for Rich Goods from the East

Wealthy Europeans began to want goods that could be obtained only by trade with distant eastern countries. Among these goods were silk and such spices as pepper, cinnamon, and cloves.

For much of the **Middle Ages** (the period from about the A.D. 400's through the 1400's), Europeans had lived simply. Nobles ran estates (large pieces of land) on which many peasants worked. Except for kings or the greatest nobles, few people enjoyed any luxuries.

In the later Middle Ages, cities began to grow. Increasing wealth and a desire for luxuries created more demand for fine goods. This demand, in turn, spurred trade.

The Spice Islands

Many of the rich goods that Europeans desired came from the East. Silk, for example, came from China. Spices, such as pepper, cinnamon, cloves, and nutmeg, came from "the Spice Islands"—a **tropical** (warm and often wet) region in what is now Indonesia. Rare jewels and porcelain (a type of ceramics) also came from the distant East.

Many merchants grew wealthy through trade with the East. Knowing that they could sell shiploads of goods at high prices, the merchants were willing to risk long, expensive voyages.

Cinnamon and cloves were among the many spices that came from the Spice Islands.

The Chinese were the world's first suppliers of silk cloth. Silk is made from the cocoons of silkworms.

A need for new trade routes

From about A.D. 1000 to 1500, European traders faced a difficult problem. The **routes** to the East were controlled by the Turks and other **Muslim** groups. Frequent wars between predominantly Christian nations of Europe and Muslim regions of the Middle East interrupted trade much of the time.

The spices and other fine goods that Europeans desired had to come by way of long land and sea voyages. Many cargoes were stolen by bandits (gangs of thieves) or pirates. Others were taken by rulers hostile to Europeans. The goods that got all the way through and ended up in European markets were precious—and very expensive.

By the 1400's, some European merchants were beginning to look for sea routes to the riches of the East. Bypassing dangerous land routes in the Middle East might be the key, they reasoned, to making big fortunes.

The Silk Road stretched across about 5,000 miles (8,050 kilometers) of mountains and deserts in central Asia and the Middle East.

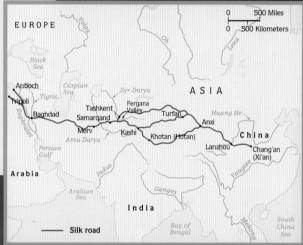

The Silk Road

The Silk Road was a group of ancient trade routes that connected China and Europe. It flourished primarily from the 100's B.C. to the A.D. 1500's. The Silk Road got its name from the Chinese silks that were carried westward on it. Travel for much of the journey was by camel caravan (a group of merchants traveling together for safety). Bandits, who had found many places to hide out, frequently attacked the caravans. In time, traders relied more on ships and less on the Silk Road.

The Known World

In the 1400's, much of the world was unknown to Europeans.

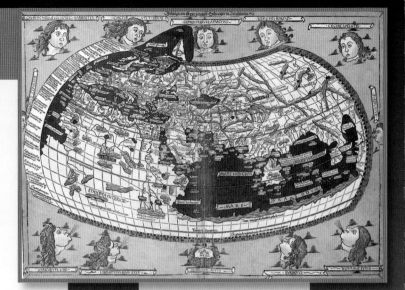

An early map of the world appeared in a 1482 edition of Ptolemy's *Geography*. The eight-volume guide to mapmaking included Ptolemy's own ideas, the work of other scholars, and travelers' reports.

It is difficult to imagine a world without television, radio, telephones, and the Internet. These means of communication make the modern world seem small, familiar, and closely tied together. In the 1400's, there was no such electronic communication. (Electronic devices use electric current to work.) Messages were sent by word of mouth or by letter. Such communications traveled only as fast as a messenger could carry them on foot, by horse, or by boat.

Without modern communications, people received very little information about distant parts of the world. To the average person, the world must have seemed a patch of familiar ground—farm, village, or town—surrounded by immense darkness.

In earlier times

The ancient Greeks and Romans also lacked modern communications. However, they greatly extended their knowledge of the world by trade, travel, and military conquest. Ptolemy *(TOL uh mee),* a Greek scientist who lived around the A.D. 100's, published a map of the world as it was known in his time. The map included Europe, northern Africa, western Asia, and parts of eastern and southern Asia.

More than 1,000 years later, the world known to Europeans was similar to Ptolemy's world map. By about 1400, Europeans had added Iceland to their map, thanks to the Vikings—but not much else.

New horizons

By the 1400's, a few brave explorers were pushing beyond the edges of the known world. However, they had no maps to guide them. Every voyage of discovery was a plunge into the unknown. Each explorer sailed a little farther into oceans and discovered unknown islands or coastlines. With each voyage, the known world expanded ever so slightly.

As the age of discovery dawned in the 1400's and 1500's, mapmaking became an important activity. Traders and explorers wanted the latest knowledge about the sea **routes** they might follow. As the map of the known world expanded, so did the imaginations of adventurous people who might themselves become explorers.

Sea Monsters

Mapmakers of the 1500's found creative ways to fill in the blank spots on their maps. They often filled uncharted (unmapped) seas with imagined sea monsters, for example. This drawing of a sea monster splashing around in the North Atlantic Ocean is from a Spanish map of 1562.

The world known to Europeans by the A.D. 1300's.

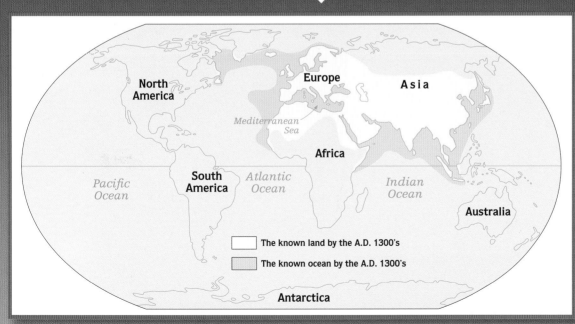

North America

Europe

Asia

Mediterranean Sea

Africa

Pacific Ocean

South America

Atlantic Ocean

Indian Ocean

Australia

☐ The known land by the A.D. 1300's

☐ The known ocean by the A.D. 1300's

Antarctica

The Portuguese Reach India

Portuguese sea captains sailed farther and farther down the west coast of Africa. In time, they went around Africa, entered the Indian Ocean, and reached India.

By 1400, some Europeans longed to travel beyond the edges of the known world. Sea traders and merchants needed faster, easier **routes** to the riches of Asia. Sailors and soldiers wanted adventure in unknown seas and new lands.

Prince Henry the Navigator

Some European rulers seized opportunities to increase their nations' wealth and power by exploration. Prince Henry the Navigator (1394–1460), a son of the king of Portugal, was one such person. (A **navigator** is a person who guides ships on sea routes.)

Prince Henry did not actually sail ships, but he encouraged and sponsored voyages of exploration down the coast of Africa. Henry hoped that sea captains would discover gold and other riches in Africa and carry them back to Portugal.

By the time of Prince Henry's death in 1460, the Portuguese had reached about one-third of the way down the western coast of Africa. Portuguese explorers continued to push farther and farther.

The Portuguese explorer Vasco da Gama commanded the first **fleet** to reach India from Europe in 1497 and 1498.

Vasco da Gama is presented to the samorin (ruler) of Kozhikode (also known as Calicut), an important trade center, upon his arrival in India in 1498.

Ships Worthy of the Ocean

Between the 1200's and the 1400's, European shipbuilders learned to build bigger and better ships for long voyages. This improved ship technology helped Vasco da Gama, Christopher Columbus, and others make successful voyages.

These explorers used ships called carracks. A carrack had high castles (raised wooden structures) at the front and back ends. It had two or three masts (long poles that support the sails) and a combination of square and triangular sails. Square sails captured the wind so that ships could move fast. Triangular sails caught the wind at odd angles so that the ship did not have to go only in the direction in which the wind was blowing.

All the way to India

In 1487, Bartolomeu Dias *(BAHR tul uh MEH oo DEE uhs)* sailed from Portugal and headed south. He went around the southern tip of Africa and into the Indian Ocean. But Dias then had to turn back.

Ten years later, in 1497, a Portuguese sea captain named Vasco da Gama rounded the southern tip of Africa and sailed across the Indian Ocean. Da Gama sailed all the way to the southwestern coast of India. This successful voyage marked a turning point in European exploration. It proved that ships could reach Asia by sailing around Africa and then across the Indian Ocean.

Vasco da Gama's historic voyage around Africa and across the Indian Ocean opened a new trade route between Europe and Asia.

The World Is Round

If the world is round, explorers reasoned, they could sail westward to reach the riches of Asia.

During the late **Middle Ages,** Europeans rediscovered scientific writings from the ancient world. Many of these works had been lost for a long time after the fall of Rome in A.D. 476. Europeans read writings by Eratosthenes *(ehr uh TOS thuh neez)*, an ancient Greek scientist. Eratosthenes said the world was a sphere (ball), and he calculated its size.

Columbus's early voyages

Christopher Columbus, born in 1451, was a ship captain and trader from the important Italian seaport of Genoa. He gained much experience sailing ships in the Mediterranean Sea and in the Atlantic Ocean. Columbus knew that Portuguese sea captains were sailing around the giant continent of Africa and across the vast Indian Ocean to reach the riches of Asia. He thought, "Why not sail westward, following the curve of the round Earth, to get to Asia?" Columbus believed that such a **route** would prove much shorter than going around Africa.

The ancient Greek scientist Eratosthenes found a way of measuring the distance around Earth without leaving northern Africa, where he lived.

Christopher Columbus, an Italian ship captain exploring for Spain, made several attempts to find a western sea route to Asia.

The Astrolabe

An astrolabe *(AS truh layb)* is an instrument that helps sailors calculate the angle of stars above the horizon. With this information, sailors at sea could figure out their **latitude.**

The astrolabe had been known to the ancient Greeks, and it was used by Islamic explorers in the Middle Ages. Europeans only came to know the astrolabe in the 1300's and 1400's.

Modern ship captains do not need to use the astrolabe. They have computers and Global Positioning Systems (GPS) to guide their ships. GPS is a worldwide **navigation** system that uses radio signals broadcast by satellites.

Columbus gets his chance

King Ferdinand and Queen Isabella of Spain were ready to listen to Columbus's ideas in early 1492. The clever explorer convinced the king and queen that he could sail straight to Asia. However, he would go west rather than east. The Spanish rulers would then be able to get rich on the goods of the East.

Ferdinand and Isabella agreed to sponsor Columbus's voyage. They provided three ships—the *Niña,* the *Pinta,* and the *Santa María.* The *Santa María* was Columbus's flagship (the ship commanded by the leader of a voyage). Ferdinand and Isabella also paid for the ships' crews and supplies, including food, water, and weapons.

Columbus's First Voyage

Christopher Columbus set sail from Spain in August 1492. His ships landed on an island off the northeastern coast of Cuba, in the New World, in October of that year.

With ships, crews, and supplies provided by the king and queen of Spain, Christopher Columbus set out from Spain in August 1492. Columbus's three ships sailed first to the Canary Islands, about 60 miles (97 kilometers) off the northwest coast of Africa. Then the ships sailed on to the west. After more than a month at sea, the crew sighted an island in the Caribbean Sea, in what are now called the West Indies. However, Columbus believed he had reached an island off the coast of Asia. He named the island *San Salvador* (Spanish for *Holy Savior*).

Columbus meets "Indians"

Native people living on the island came out to greet their unexpected visitors. Scholars believe that the islanders were from a tribe of Arawak people called the Taíno. But Columbus called them Indians because he believed that he was in the East Indies—a large group of islands off the southeastern coast of Asia. As it turned out, the name *Indian* was based on a mistake. But it stuck.

Columbus kidnapped several of the Taíno. He would take them back to Spain with his ships and crew.

Replicas of the *Niña*, the *Pinta*, and the *Santa María*—the three ships Columbus commanded on his voyage across the Atlantic Ocean in 1492—reenact the voyage in 1991.

The first landing of Christopher Columbus in America as imagined by the Spanish painter Dióscoro Teófilo Puebla Tolín (1831-1901).

Further exploration

Columbus then guided his ships on to the west. Soon, the ships reached the north coast of Cuba. The ships explored part of Cuba's northern coast as they turned back to the east. Then the ships reached an island that Columbus called Hispaniola. Today this island is divided between the nations of the Dominican Republic and Haiti.

On December 25, 1492, Columbus's flagship was wrecked on a reef (an offshore ridge of jagged rock) along the coast of Hispaniola. Columbus and most of his crew escaped to shore.

Return to Spain

With the *Santa María* wrecked, Columbus and his crew returned to Spain aboard the *Niña* and the *Pinta*. The ships arrived in Spain in mid-March of 1493, after a two-month voyage. Columbus had been unable to bring back a cargo of riches. But some trinkets and the "Indians" he displayed convinced King Ferdinand and Queen Isabella that Columbus had, indeed, reached Asia. They were eager to send him on another **expedition.**

How Columbus Did It

Most historians consider Columbus to have been a talented **navigator.** To guide his ships, Columbus used these instruments and methods:

- A quadrant—a simple version of an astrolabe—allowed Columbus to calculate the angle of the North Star. With this information, he could figure out **latitude.**

- A compass enabled Columbus to set and keep to his course.

- A sand-filled hourglass helped Columbus keep time.

- There was no speedometer in Columbus's day, so he guessed at the ship's speed. Columbus was a very experienced ship captain, so he was quite good at estimating speed.

On his first voyage, Columbus sailed from Spain to the Canary Islands, then west until he hit land on San Salvador Island. He explored the islands of Cuba and Hispaniola before returning to Spain.

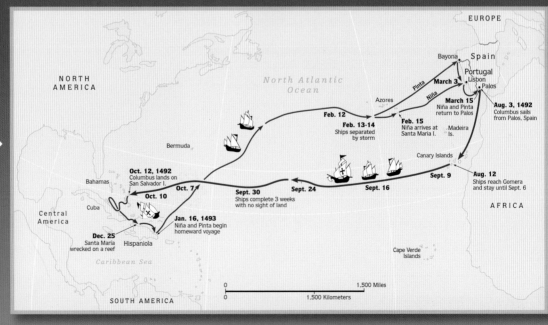

Columbus's Later Voyages

After his voyage of discovery in 1492, Columbus made three more trips to the New World. Although he discovered new lands, Columbus failed to find Asia.

Across the Atlantic—again

King Ferdinand and Queen Isabella of Spain quickly made arrangements to send Columbus on another voyage to the lands in the west. They provided a large **fleet** of 17 ships, crew members, and colonists to settle the lands discovered by Columbus. Columbus's fleet left Spain in September 1493. It arrived in Hispaniola about three weeks later.

Columbus built **forts** (strong buildings that can be defended) in Hispaniola and settled the colonists there. On this voyage, Columbus also discovered the islands of Puerto Rico and Jamaica. Meanwhile, things did not go well in the colony on Hispaniola. The colonists fought among themselves, and they fought with the native Taíno. Columbus appointed his brothers Bartholomew and Diego to rule the colony. The brothers treated the Taíno harshly.

Columbus then explored much of the coastline of Cuba. Although he probably realized it was a big island, he insisted that it was the coast of Asia. He still wanted King Ferdinand and Queen Isabella to think he had reached the East.

Columbus found it necessary to return to Spain in 1496. Some colonists from Hispaniola had already returned and complained to the Spanish king and queen about the harsh rule of Columbus and his brothers. In addition, some priests criticized the maltreatment of the Taíno.

Columbus's tomb is on display at Seville Cathedral in Seville, Spain.

The third voyage

Columbus departed from Spain again in May 1498. This time he sailed farther south. In July, he reached the island of Trinidad, just off the northern coast of South America. Then he explored the coast of what is now Venezuela and eventually set sail for Hispaniola.

Upon arriving on the island, Columbus discovered that conditions had worsened. In August 1500, a Spanish official sent by Ferdinand and Isabella arrested Columbus and his brothers and sent them back to Spain for trial. As always, the king and queen forgave Columbus and sent him on a new **expedition.**

The fourth voyage

Columbus set sail from Spain in May 1502 for his fourth—and final—voyage. He explored unknown lands on the western end of the Caribbean Sea. These included the coastlines of present-day Honduras, Nicaragua, Costa Rica, and Panama. While returning to the Spanish base at Hispaniola, Columbus and his crew became marooned (stranded) on the island of Jamaica. Their ships were in such bad shape that they were no longer seaworthy. The explorers had to wait on Jamaica for a year until ships could rescue them. Columbus then returned to Spain, arriving in November 1504. He died at his home in Spain on May 20, 1506.

A West Indies Hurricane

In June 1502, Columbus's ships were caught in a hurricane off the coast of Hispaniola. Columbus's ships survived the storm, but all but one of the 21 ships sent out by the governor of Hispaniola sank.

A hurricane is a huge, swirling storm that forms over **tropical** oceans and sometimes hits land. Before the Age of Exploration, Europeans were probably unfamiliar with these dangerous storms.

Columbus explored several islands in the West Indies on three separate voyages between 1493 and 1504.

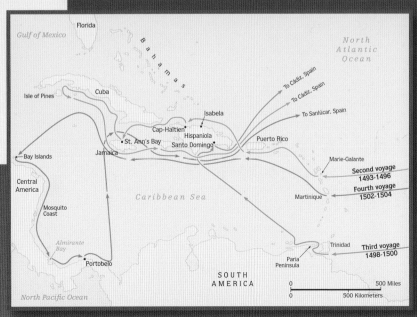

Amerigo Vespucci

Columbus was the most famous explorer of the Western Hemisphere. But another Italian sea captain became the namesake for the New World.

Columbus returned from his first voyage in 1493 with stories of his landings far to the west—in "Asia." The news spread like wildfire. Adventurous sea captains began to ask the Spanish king and queen and other European rulers to sponsor their voyages of discovery.

The New World gets a name

Amerigo Vespucci *(uh MEHR uh GOH veh SPOO chee)* was—like Columbus—an Italian sea captain. Vespucci claimed that he had led an **expedition** to the **New World** (the Americas) in 1497 and discovered the continent of South America.

In 1502 or 1503, Vespucci wrote a vivid description of South America, which he identified as a new continent. Vespucci's description was published under the title *Mundus Novus (New World).* Many educated Europeans read Vespucci's book and were convinced that he was the discoverer of the "new world" across the ocean.

One European who read *Mundus Novus* was German mapmaker Martin Waldseemüller. In 1507, he published a map of the world. On his map, Waldseemüller labeled the New World lands as "America," in honor of Amerigo Vespucci. Soon this name was used widely.

Later, most people became aware that Christopher Columbus had actually been the first explorer to reach the West Indies in the New World. But the name *America* stuck.

▲ Amerigo Vespucci was an Italian-born explorer for whom America is named.

Setting the record straight

Most historians doubt Vespucci's claim that he was the discoverer of South America. They find no evidence that Vespucci was in the New World as early as 1497. However, they have uncovered evidence that Vespucci sailed with the Spanish explorer Alonso de Ojeda between 1499 and 1500 and with the Portuguese explorer Gonçalo Coelho in 1501 and 1502 and again in 1503 and 1504. Both of these explorers sailed along the coasts of South America. Historians believe that Vespucci may have taken careful notes of everything he saw while on these journeys.

Historical records prove that Christopher Columbus discovered South America on his third voyage in 1498. If Vespucci's claim of seeing South America on a voyage in 1497 is false, as historians believe, then Columbus is surely the first European discoverer of the continent.

What's in a Name?

If Amerigo Vespucci had not been the first explorer to publish a book about the New World, the newly discovered continents would probably have been named for Columbus. However, many places in the Americas were named for Columbus. Here is a sampling:

- the nation of Colombia in South America
- the province of British Columbia in Canada
- the District of Columbia, the U.S. capital
- the city of Colón in Panama
- many U.S. towns and cities named "Columbus," including the capital of Ohio
- many U.S. towns and cities named "Columbia," including the capital of South Carolina

Martin Waldseemüller's 1507 map of the world was the first document known to name America.

Magellan and del Cano Sail Around the World

In 1519, Ferdinand Magellan began an expedition around the world. Juan Sebastian del Cano completed the voyage after Magellan died.

Ferdinand Magellan was a Portuguese sailor. After serving as a crew member on a number of voyages, he studied to become a ship **navigator.** Like Christopher Columbus, Magellan had big ideas. He believed that an **expedition** could sail around the southern tip of South America and beyond to the Spice Islands of Asia. Magellan spent years trying to persuade rulers to give him financial support. Finally, in 1518, King Charles I of Spain agreed to sponsor his expedition.

The expedition begins

In September 1519, Magellan set sail from Spain with his flagship, *Trinidad,* and four other ships. Magellan's expedition crossed the Atlantic Ocean and then sailed down the east coast of South America. After spending several months in what is now Argentina, Magellan's ships set sail again in October 1520. During that month, the expedition found the sea passage through the southern tip of South America from the Atlantic Ocean to the western ocean. Ever since, this passage has been known as the Strait of Magellan. In November, three of Magellan's ships sailed into this western ocean. Magellan named it *Pacific,* meaning "peaceful."

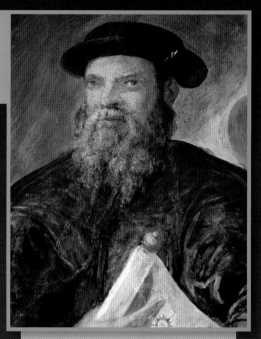

Ferdinand Magellan led the first expedition that sailed around the world between 1519 and 1522.

At the Same Time...

Great events were taking place in Europe around the time of Magellan's expedition around the globe. In 1517, a German monk (one who leads a life of prayer) named Martin Luther made public a list that criticized the Roman Catholic Church. In 1520, he wrote three books stating his views on Christianity. His actions started the Protestant Reformation, which called for a return to a Christianity based more closely on the Bible. As a result, Europe—and later the Americas—became divided into Catholic and Protestant camps.

Travel Then and Now

Magellan's ships covered nearly 10,000 miles (about 16,100 kilometers) of open water as they crossed the Pacific in late 1520 and early 1521. Sailing from the southern tip of South America to the island of Guam took almost 100 days. Today, large commercial jet planes can travel this distance in about 20 hours.

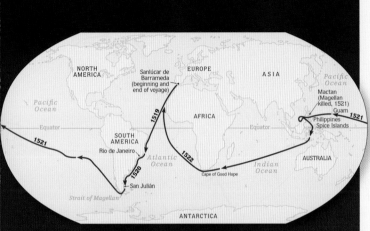

Magellan's search for a western passage to the Pacific Ocean and the Spice Islands resulted in the first round-the-world voyage.

Magellan died battling native peoples on the island of Mactan in 1521.

The wide Pacific

No one had ever before sailed across the Pacific Ocean, and no one knew how large it was. Magellan's ships sailed for almost 100 days before reaching the island of Guam in the western Pacific. During that time, Magellan's crew ran out of food and began eating hides, sawdust, and rats. In all, 19 men starved to death. On Guam, Magellan was able to partly resupply his ships.

Magellan's death

The expedition then sailed to the Philippine Islands. Magellan established a base there and began converting natives to Christianity. However, Magellan died battling rival Filipino groups on April 27, 1521.

After Magellan's death, Sebastian del Cano commanded the ship *Victoria* and sailed it back to Spain. The *Victoria,* the only one of Magellan's ships to return, arrived in Sanlúcar de Barrameda, Spain, on September 6, 1522. Del Cano returned with only 17 crew members—out of the original crew of about 240.

Magellan's voyage of 1519–1522 is a milestone in world history. It marked the very first time that people traveled all the way around the world. Magellan discovered lands and seas previously unknown to Europeans, and he proved that it was possible to sail westward from Europe to the Spice Islands of Asia.

The Spaniards Conquer Mexico

Spanish explorers soon discovered and conquered a rich prize—Mexico.

Columbus and other European sea captains explored islands in the West Indies and set up Spanish colonies there. In time, Spanish explorers began to look beyond these islands to land masses north, west, and south of the West Indies.

Cortés explores Mexico

In 1519, a Spanish explorer named Hernán Cortés *(kawr TEHZ)* led a force of 600 soldiers from the island of Cuba to what is now the coast of Mexico. Cortés and his soldiers marched along the coast and then turned inland, away from the sea. They had heard rumors of fabulous cities and wealth.

Cortés gained help from some Indian tribes who were enemies of the Aztec, the most powerful tribe of Mexico. He also received help from an Indian woman named Malinche who translated Aztec and other Indian languages into Spanish and Spanish into the Indian languages.

The Aztec Empire

The Aztec Empire was rich and powerful. It was ruled from the capital city of Tenochtitlan *(tay nohch TEE tlahn)* by Montezuma II. Tenochtitlan was a dazzling city of about 200,000 to 300,000 people, larger than any Spanish city of that time.

Hernán Cortés was a Spanish explorer who conquered what is now central and southern Mexico in the early 1500's.

The Spaniards arrive

Hearing that Cortés and his soldiers were on their way to Tenochtitlan, Montezuma sent messengers with rich gifts for Cortés, along with a message ordering the Spaniards to leave. Instead, Cortés and his army entered the city, captured Montezuma, and held him prisoner.

In June 1520, the Aztec rebelled against their occupiers. During the battle, Montezuma was killed. The Aztec drove the invaders from their city, but not for long. In December 1520, Cortés and his soldiers returned to Tenochtitlan. For months, the Spaniards surrounded the city, cutting off food and water supplies. In August 1521, the new Aztec emperor, Cuauhtémoc, surrendered the city.

New Spain

The Spaniards set up their colony of New Spain in place of the Aztec Empire. They destroyed Tenochtitlan and built Mexico City on top of the ruins. They demanded that the Indian peoples convert to the Catholic religion. The Aztec religion had included human sacrifice, which the Spaniards condemned. However, the Spanish conquerors committed many acts of cruelty against the native people of Mexico.

An illustration from a manuscript made in the late 1500's shows native peoples welcoming Cortés to Mexico.

An artist's rendering of Tenochtitlan shows the grand architecture of the ancient city on which Mexico City would be built.

The Spaniards Conquer Peru

Spanish explorers conquered the powerful Inca Empire and founded Peru.

In the early 1500's, Spaniards began to explore southward into the continent of South America. In 1513, a Spanish explorer named Vasco Núñez de Balboa *(VAHS koh NOO nyayth day bal BOH uh)* crossed the isthmus of Panama and looked out over the vast Pacific Ocean. (An isthmus is a narrow strip of land that connects two larger bodies of land.) In time, other explorers followed the Pacific coastline down the western coast of South America.

Pizarro's expeditions

Francisco Pizarro, an explorer who had been with Balboa in 1513, heard stories of a rich, powerful **empire** far to the south. Pizarro, already rich from Spanish conquests and plunder, was eager to conquer new empires. He launched his first **expedition** in 1524. Pizarro did not at first find empires or riches. But he continued to explore, pushing a bit farther south along the west coast of South America on each voyage.

Finally, in 1527 or early 1528, Pizarro reached the coast of present-day Peru, which was then territory belonging to the Inca. The Inca, a native American people, controlled a great empire along the west coast of South America.

Vasco Núñez de Balboa was the first European to see the eastern shore of the Pacific Ocean. On September 29, 1513, he waded into the ocean and claimed it and all its shores for Spain.

Beginning in 1524, the Spanish explorer Francisco Pizarro made several journeys along the northwestern coast of South America.

The Inca Empire

The Inca had built a great empire both by conquering other Indian tribes and by making alliances (treaties of friendship) with some tribes. They tied their vast empire together by building a network of roads. The Inca built great stone structures and cities. They also made beautiful objects out of such precious metals as gold and silver. The Inca capital city, Cusco, and Machu Picchu, a royal city high in the mountains, especially impressed the Spanish invaders.

In 1532, Pizarro and his men launched a surprise attack against the Inca with swords, horses, and guns. They captured the Inca ruler, Atahualpa *(AH tah WAHL pah)*, and killed thousands of Inca. Pizarro then demanded a ransom (money in exchange for the release of a prisoner) of silver and gold from Inca nobles. Pizarro received the silver and gold—and then killed Atahualpa. The Spaniards were then able to conquer the leaderless Inca Empire.

The founding of Peru

Pizarro created the Spanish colony of Peru and founded its capital city, Lima, in 1535. Pizarro died in Peru at the hand of a rival Spanish explorer in 1541.

Cortés and Pizarro had secured great prizes for Spain in the colonies of New Spain (Mexico) and Peru. Gold and silver were shipped back to Spain. These treasures greatly enriched the Spanish king and queen and many Spanish nobles.

Inca craftworkers created fine works of art, such as these silver llamas and female figurines.

World famous Machu Picchu is the ruins of a mountaintop settlement that is believed to have been a summer palace of the Inca royal family.

The Spaniards Explore and Colonize

During the 1500's and 1600's, Spaniards explored and settled much of South America, Central America, and southern North America.

Mexico and Peru were Spain's greatest prizes in the **New World,** but Spaniards explored many other regions, too. They settled most of the Caribbean Islands, the areas that Columbus had visited in his voyages. Some of the most important Spanish settlements were on the islands of Cuba, Hispaniola, and Puerto Rico.

The North American mainland

In 1513, Juan Ponce de León *(hwahn PAWN say day lay AWN* or *PAWNS duh LEE awhn)* sailed from Puerto Rico and landed on the east coast of Florida. He named the land *La Florida,* probably because he arrived there during the season of Easter, which the Spaniards called *Pascua Florida* (Easter of the Flowers). In 1521, Ponce de León tried to start a colony in Florida. But before long, the colonists fled to Cuba.

Juan Ponce de León, a Spanish explorer, led the first recorded European expedition to reach what is now Florida.

De Soto's expedition

In 1539, the Spanish explorer Hernando de Soto led an **expedition** to what is now the south-eastern United States. He landed on the west coast of Florida near present-day Tampa Bay. After spending a winter in northern Florida, De Soto and his army traveled through the present-day states of Georgia, the Carolinas, Tennessee, and Alabama. In 1541, De Soto became the first European to see the Mississippi River. He died on the banks of the river on May 21, 1542.

Hernando de Soto's explorations in the American Southeast.

Exploring the Southwest

In 1540, another Spaniard, Francisco Vásquez de Coronado, led an expedition from western Mexico northward into the interior of what is today the western United States. Coronado did not find the riches he was seeking, but he became the first European to travel through the American Southwest.

From the 1560's to the 1820's, Spanish missionaries established themselves among the Indians in the regions between Florida and California. Their aim was to convert Indians to Christianity.

Southern South America

Spanish explorers also pushed farther down the east coast of South America. In 1516, Juan Díaz de Solís was searching for a southern sea passage through South America that, he hoped, would lead to the Pacific Ocean. Solis was disappointed to discover that the broad river he named Río de la Plata did not lead to the Pacific, but he claimed the area for Spain. Later, the great city of Buenos Aires, Argentina, was founded on the river's bank.

The Gentle Priest

Many Spanish explorers and governors gained reputations for cruelty in their dealings with the Indians. But not all Spaniards in the New World treated Indians harshly. A Catholic priest named Bartolomé de Las Casas *(BAHR toh loh MAY day lahs KAH sahs)* tried hard to improve conditions for the Indians. For many years, the gentle priest lived on the island of Hispaniola, where he saw first-hand how poorly the Indians were treated. In many writings, Las Casas called for fair treatment of the Indians.

Buenos Aires, Argentina's capital and largest city, has a mixture of modern skyscrapers and Spanish colonial buildings. ❯

The Portuguese Settle Brazil

One region of the Americas, the South American nation of Brazil, was colonized by the Portuguese.

In the late 1400's, both Spain and its small neighbor, Portugal, were heavily involved in exploration by sea. Explorers of both countries were seeking new sea **routes** to the riches of the East. After Columbus returned from his first voyage in 1493, Pope Alexander VI, the powerful head of the Roman Catholic Church, divided the world between Spain and Portugal for future exploration. This "line of demarcation" gave Portugal the right to explore and colonize eastern South America as well as Africa, the Indian Ocean, and parts of Asia.

Cabral reaches Brazil

In 1500, a Portuguese **expedition** led by Pedro Álvares Cabral went off course as the ships sailed down the coast of Africa en route to India. Cabral's ships instead reached the eastern tip of South America. Cabral claimed the land for Portugal. Cabral's Portuguese sailors called the new land *Brazil,* a name they formed out of the Portuguese word *brasa,* meaning "glowing ember." (An ember is a piece of wood or coal that glows red-hot after a fire dies down.) The explorers had noticed that the wood of certain trees they saw had the bright, deep color of glowing embers.

During the mid-1500's, many Portuguese colonists came to northeastern Brazil and established large sugar cane plantations. They brought African slaves to work on these plantations.

Pope Alexander VI hoped that his line of demarcation would prevent disputes between Spain and Portugal over new lands discovered by explorers.

The Amazon

Much of northern Brazil is a huge rain forest surrounding the Amazon River and its tributaries (streams that flow into it). The Amazon is the second longest river in the world. Only the Nile River is longer. However, the Amazon carries more water to the ocean than any other river.

In 1541, a Spanish expedition set out eastward from Quito, a settlement near the west coast of South America, into the mysterious interior of South America. After crossing high mountains, the expedition traveled down tributaries of the Amazon and, finally, the Amazon itself. Francisco de Orellana *(OH ray YAH nah)* broke away from the main expedition, leading a group of men in boats all the way east to the mouth of the Amazon at the Atlantic Ocean.

During Orellana's journey, what appeared to be female Indian warriors attacked his crew. The Spaniards called their attackers Amazons. In Greek myths, an Amazon is a powerful woman warrior. The name *Amazon* later was given to the river and nearby area.

Colonists

In the 1530's, Portuguese colonists began to settle Brazil. It became a rich and successful colony. Today, the independent nation of Brazil is by far the largest Portuguese-speaking nation in the world. Its population in 2010 was about 193 million.

The Amazon River is the world's second longest river.

Did You Know?

Portuguese and Spanish are closely related languages. However, without special study, speakers of Spanish and Portuguese cannot understand each other. Both languages developed from Latin, the language of the **Roman Empire.** Over many centuries, people in Portugal and parts of Spain began to speak Latin quite differently.

The Slave Trade

As Europeans were settling the New World, they enslaved many thousands of African people and shipped them to American colonies.

Most African slaves were kidnapped from along the west coast of Africa, then sold by Arab traders to European merchants, who transported them to the Americas.

European colonists found that they needed many workers for farming, mining, and other activities in the **New World.** At first, they forced the local Indians to work for them. However, many of the Indians died of diseases brought by the Europeans. European traders then turned to Africans to supply labor in the New World.

Arab traders began enslaving black Africans during the late **Middle Ages.** During the 1400's, Portuguese traders began enslaving blacks, too. They shipped African blacks to Europe as slaves. The Portuguese also enslaved blacks on sugar plantations (large farms where workers usually grow a single crop) that they established on islands off the coast of West Africa.

Plantations in the New World

Adventurous Europeans eager to get rich followed the explorers to the New World. Spaniards and Portuguese started plantations on some Caribbean islands and in Brazil. In these hot places, sugar cane grew well. Europeans were developing a taste for refined sugar, which had previously been absent from most of their diets. Sugar, therefore, became one of the most profitable (money-making) crops. Many European planters became rich from sugar production. As they worked more land, they purchased ever more slaves.

Raising and processing sugar cane required slaves to work very hard in difficult conditions. Many slaves fell sick and died. The plantation owners then simply bought more slaves to replace them.

Slavery spreads northward

Eventually, colonies developed farther north on the North American mainland. The climates of these places supported such crops as tobacco, rice, indigo (a plant dye), and cotton. African slaves were brought to these colonies, too, to provide labor for field work and for other jobs. Now, many of the enslaved Africans were transported by English, Dutch, French, or American merchants.

Africans in the New World

The slave trade lasted from the 1500's to the early 1800's. As a result of slavery, the population of the Americas today includes many people of African descent (ancestry). Today, black people make up the majority in Haiti and Jamaica and some other Caribbean countries. People of African descent and mixed ancestry make up about two-thirds of the population of Cuba and nearly half of that of Brazil. About 12 percent of the population of the United States is classified as black or African American.

Africans were packed tightly aboard slave ships. They endured such harsh conditions on the voyage across the Atlantic Ocean that many died.

The Search for a Northwest Passage

In the early 1500's, Europeans concluded that Columbus had discovered new continents to the west. They realized that Asia lay still farther west beyond the New World. Explorers then began to search for a sea passage around or through the northern part of North America.

Some explorers reasoned that getting around or through the new continents would put them on the path to Asia's riches. They suspected that a sea passage might be found along the northern coasts of North America. They referred to such a **route** as the Northwest Passage.

Seeking the passage

The English sea captain Sir Martin Frobisher sailed westward from England along a northerly route in 1576. He reached Greenland and sailed around the southern tip of the huge island. He then sailed on to Baffin Island and discovered the bay that now bears his name. Frobisher made two later voyages in search of the Northwest Passage.

John Davis, another talented English sea captain, also looked for the Northwest Passage. From 1585 to 1587, he headed three **expeditions** to northwestern North America. Davis explored the wide strait between Greenland and Baffin Island. (A strait is a narrow waterway connecting two larger bodies of water.) It is now called the Davis Strait.

Other explorers probed bodies of water in northwestern North America for the passage. In each case, they returned home believing that there could be a passage—but they had failed to find it.

Sir Martin Frobisher was one of the first English explorers to seek a Northwest Passage to India and eastern Asia.

During two voyages to North America, Henry Hudson explored the waterways known today as the Hudson River, Hudson Bay, and Hudson Strait.

Henry Hudson's voyages

Henry Hudson, an English explorer, led two voyages to North America searching for the Northwest Passage. In 1609, Hudson crossed the Atlantic and sailed along the east coast of what is now the United States. He discovered and explored what is now known as the Hudson River in the present-day state of New York.

In 1610, Hudson led a second expedition to North America. Hudson arrived at the coast of Labrador, in what is now Canada. He then steered his ship through a narrow body of water we now know as the Hudson Strait.

At its western end, the Hudson Strait opens into Hudson Bay. Seeing this enormous body of water, Hudson believed that he had found the Pacific Ocean.

During the winter months of 1611, Hudson's ship became trapped in ice. When the bay thawed in the spring, Hudson's crew rebelled and set Hudson adrift in a small boat. Hudson's ship and crew returned to England—but the explorer was never heard from again.

Is There a Northwest Passage?

There is a Northwest Passage. It is through the Arctic Ocean and other waters around the top of North America. However, some of these waters are frozen year-round. Today, some scientists predict that the Northwest Passage may become navigable in the future. A steady rise in Earth's temperature since the 1700's is causing Arctic ice to melt partially during summer months.

Henry Hudson made four voyages in an attempt to discover a northern route between Europe and Asia.

Exploration Changes Life in the Americas

The Age of Exploration dramatically changed ways of life in the New World.

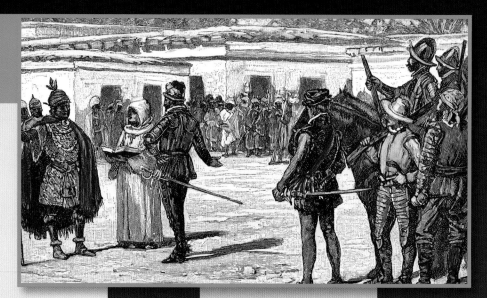

A dying time

No one knows how many native people lived in the **New World** when Christopher Columbus first arrived in 1492. But many historians estimate that there were tens of millions of natives living in the Americas at that time.

The European explorers and colonists brought devastating plagues (deadly diseases) to the New World. Europeans had long suffered from such diseases as measles and smallpox. However, the natives of the Americas had never before been exposed to such disease. They had no natural immunity (resistance) to the European diseases.

No one will ever know how many Indians died of disease during the Age of Exploration. Many historians estimate that millions of Indians were felled by diseases common to Europeans.

Spanish explorer Francisco Pizarro greets Inca leader Atahualpa. Europeans brought violence and disease to the New World, devastating native populations across the Americas.

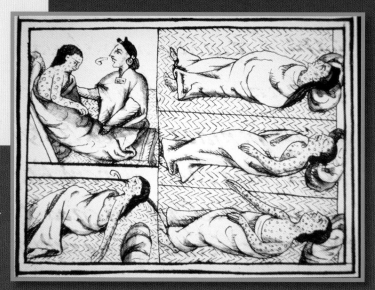

An illustrated manuscript from the 1500's depicts the terrible effects of smallpox on native peoples. ❯

Vanishing Native American cultures

Even as native populations shrank due to European diseases, explorers and colonists continually arrived in the New World. In time, these colonizing Europeans overwhelmed some Indian tribes and pushed others into interiors away from coastlines.

As the twin disasters of plagues and European violence spread, some Indian tribes ceased to exist. Others suffered sharply reduced numbers and scarce resources. In some cases, Indian tribes were relocated (moved to places far from their original homelands). These pressures wiped out advanced American Indian societies, such as the Aztec and the Inca. Many parts of these cultures were lost.

New societies and cultures

The colonizing Europeans created new societies and cultures in the New World. Some were strongly influenced by Spain or Portugal; others by Britain or France. In time, all of these societies evolved into new forms that mixed European, American Indian, and African sources. Many societies in the New World came to be called "melting pots." These societies were among the first to create the diversity (varieties of ethnic groups) that has become a hallmark of the modern world.

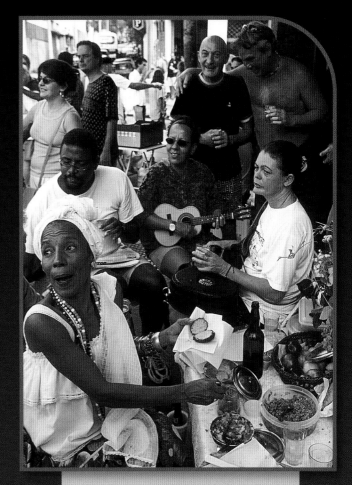

The Americas are home to a diverse group of ethnicities and cultures due to European colonization.

Alejandro Toledo was the first democratically elected Peruvian president of American Indian ancestry. He served as president of Peru from 2001 to 2006. **>**

Exploration Changes Life in Europe

The Age of Exploration changed ways of life in Europe, too.

New foods

According to legend, Spanish colonists returning from the **New World** in the 1540's presented containers of a frothy chocolate beverage to Prince Philip of Spain. The Spaniards soon found that adding sugar to the bitter chocolate gave it a pleasing flavor. Within several decades, chocolate became a food fad across Europe.

Chocolate is only one example of a food that Europeans received from the New World. Explorers sailed to Europe with cargoes of strange edible plants. In time, European farmers cultivated many of these food crops for their local markets. Among them were avocados, corn (also called maize), peanuts, peppers, potatoes, sweet potatoes, squashes, and tomatoes.

Some New World foods, in time, became staples of European diets. (A staple is a food on which people depend heavily.) For example, corn became an important grain crop in Italy, where it is used to make a food called polenta. Potatoes became an important staple in Ireland, Germany, and other countries. Tomatoes, widely used in Europe, are especially popular in Spanish and Italian dishes.

Another American crop, tobacco, soon became known in Europe. It started the fad of smoking.

European explorers brought corn and other American crops back to their homeland.

European empires

Contact with the New World and colonization there brought about many other changes to European life. Control of large new regions and their resources made certain countries in Europe wealthier and more powerful than they had been before. At first, Spain and Portugal built up world **empires** and gained great riches. Later, France and England began setting up colonies in the New World. They, too, built great empires.

Cargoes of gold and silver

Some European nations with New World colonies began to import (bring into their home countries) large amounts of gold and silver. Nations with large supplies of precious metals could pay higher and higher prices for precious goods. Prices for all kinds of goods then soared. These developments triggered a long period of inflation (rapid price increases) in Europe's **economies.**

The wealthiest Europeans were able to pay higher prices for items necessary to life. But the poorest Europeans suffered greatly during this era. They had difficulty buying the basics—food, clothing, and shelter.

Words, Words, Words

Many words we use in English today have their origin in languages of American Indians. Here is a sampling.

English Word	Source (Indian Tribe)
chipmunk	Ojibwa
chocolate	Nahuatl of Mexico
hickory	Algonquian
kayak	Inuit of Greenland
moccasin	Algonquian
moose	Algonquian
pecan	Algonquian or Cree
squash	Narragansett

The necklace of the Knight of the Order of the Golden Fleece was created for members of the French royal court around 1550. In this era, jewelry was worn by royalty and members of the middle class.

The English Explore the Atlantic Seacoast

England sent explorers and, later, colonists to the Atlantic seacoast of North America.

Word of Spanish and Portuguese voyages of discovery spread quickly throughout Europe. Rulers of other countries were determined not be left out of the race for lands and treasure.

In 1496, King Henry VII of England hired an Italian sea captain to lead an **expedition** westward across the sea to Asia. The sea captain's Italian name was Zuan Chabotto, but he became known in England as John Cabot. Cabot sailed westward with one ship from Bristol, England, in May 1497. He landed on the coast of what is now Newfoundland, Canada, and returned to England in August. Cabot set out on a second voyage in 1498. This time, Cabot, his crew, and ships were lost at sea.

The Lost Colony

In 1585, a British explorer and businessman named Sir Walter Raleigh attempted to establish the first colony in what is now the United States. He sent settlers to Roanoke Island, off the coast of North Carolina. After many of the settlers returned to England, Raleigh sent more colonists to the island. By July 1587, the colony consisted of 117 people.

War in Europe prevented supply ships from returning to the colony from England for three years. When English ships finally returned to the Roanoke colony in 1590, all of the colonists had vanished.

This map shows John Cabot's voyage from England to North America in 1497.

What Happened to the Lost Colony?

People have long been fascinated by the Lost Colony. Each summer, thousands of tourists attend a pageant (outdoor performance of a historical play) in Manteo, North Carolina, that tells the story of the doomed colony.

The only traces of the colonists were the letters *CRO* and the word *Croatoan* carved onto two separate trees. The Croatan were an Indian tribe who lived near Roanoke Island.

Some modern historians think that most of the lost colonists may have moved to Chesapeake Bay and perished there in conflicts with Indians. Stories collected by Virginians indicate that other members of the Lost Colony may have mingled with several Indian tribes. Today, many Lumbee Indians believe that they are descendants of the Croatan and the lost colonists and of Indians who lived nearby.

The Jamestown colony

The English were not ready to give up their claims to North America. In 1607, the Virginia Company of London sent three ships with crews, supplies, and colonists to the Chesapeake Bay region. (The Virginia Company of London was a group of important English merchants, politicians, and nobles.) The colonists settled at Jamestown in what is now the state of Virginia. Although the colony got off to a shaky start, it held on.

Plymouth Bay and Massachusetts

In 1620, a group of English dissenters (Protestants who did not support the official Church of England) sailed to America for religious freedom. They landed on the coast of present-day Massachusetts and started the Plymouth colony. In time, thousands more English colonists came to Massachusetts, and the colony thrived.

Thirteen Colonies

Between 1623 and 1733, English colonists settled 11 more colonies in what is now the United States. Eventually, the English controlled much of North America. They also established some colonies in the Caribbean.

What's in a Name?

The English explorers who first visited the middle Atlantic coast of North America named the region "Virginia." Later this became the name of a colony—and still later—of a state. The explorers wanted to honor their queen, Elizabeth I. She was known as the "Virgin" queen because she never married. Elizabeth believed that she needed to remain free of a husband to be a good ruler. Her decision not to marry was highly unusual for a reigning queen of her time.

In 1620, a group of English colonists arrived at Plymouth Bay aboard the *Mayflower*. *Mayflower II* was built as the original ship is thought to have looked. ❯

The French Explore North America

French explorers traveled around much of inland North America. They started the colonies of New France and Louisiana.

The rulers of France, another powerful country in Europe, wanted a share in **New World** exploration. In 1524, King Francis I sent Giovanni da Verrazzano *(joh VAHN ee dah VEHR uh ZAH noh)* westward on a voyage of exploration. The French king hoped that Verrazzano would find a sea passage through American lands to the Asian lands beyond. Verrazzano explored much of the eastern coast of North America, but he did not find a passage.

Between 1534 and 1536, a French explorer named Jacques Cartier *(zhahk kahr TYAY)* explored a major river in present-day Canada and claimed the land for France. He named the river the St. Lawrence, after a Roman Catholic saint. Cartier sailed up the St. Lawrence as far as present-day Montreal—more than 500 miles (805 kilometers) inland.

A new colony

In the early 1600's, another French explorer, Samuel de Champlain *(sham PLAYN),* led a number of **expeditions** to the New World. Champlain went deeper into northern North America than other Europeans at that time. He was the first to see the Great Lakes and Niagara Falls. He discovered many other lakes and many rivers in the interior of North America.

In 1608, Champlain founded the city of Quebec. It was the first permanent settlement in France's colony of New France.

▲ Jacques Cartier's explorations established the basis for France's claims to territory in what is now Canada.

Samuel de Champlain explored the St. Lawrence River, parts of the North American coast, and the Great Lakes region from 1603 to 1615.

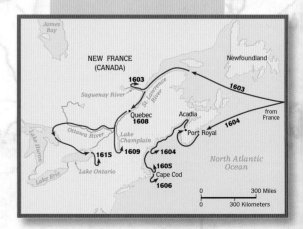

Into the heart of North America

Later in the 1600's, French explorers followed rivers and lakes all the way to the middle of North America. In 1673, Louis Jolliet *(lwee JOH lee eht)* and Jacques Marquette *(mahr KEHT)* explored the northern part of the Mississippi River. Europeans had never before visited this region. Marquette and Jolliet used canoes to paddle up and down rivers. In some places, they had to carry the canoes across land between rivers. The French explorers learned how to make canoes from Indians living along the rivers and lakes of North America.

Down the Mississippi

Jolliet and Marquette paddled down the Mississippi as far as the place where the Arkansas River flows into it. This is a distance of more than 700 miles (1,127 kilometers).

In 1682, René-Robert Cavelier, Sieur de La Salle *(ruh nay roh behr kah vahl yay, syur duh luh sal)* led an expedition down the Illinois and Mississippi rivers. He went all the way to the mouth of the Mississippi on the Gulf of Mexico. La Salle claimed the lands drained by the Mississippi River for France. He named the region Louisiana in honor of King Louis XIV of France.

In 1718, the French founded the city of New Orleans near the mouth of the Mississippi River. It became the capital of the Louisiana colony.

Did You Know?

The opening between the Atlantic Ocean and New York City harbor was named the Verrazano Narrows in honor of the explorer Giovanni da Verrazzano. In 1964, a bridge was built across the narrows to connect two boroughs (sections) of New York City. Called the Verrazano-Narrows Bridge, it is one of the largest suspension bridges in the world. In a suspension bridge, the roadbed is supported by thick, strong cables.

La Salle explored the interior of North America in the late 1600's.

The Dutch Explore America and Asia

The Dutch started an American colony in what is now the state of New York. They also set up colonies in southern Africa and on islands that now form part of Indonesia.

The small country known as the Netherlands (sometimes called Holland) was not as powerful as England or France. However, some of its people were expert sea captains. People of the Netherlands, called the Dutch, depended heavily on foreign trade, especially sea trade. They were interested in starting colonies because colonies would increase overseas trade.

New Netherland

Henry Hudson discovered the Hudson River in 1609 and claimed it for the Netherlands. Hudson had been hired for this voyage by the Dutch West India Company, a group of Dutch investors in West Indies trade and colonization. In 1624, the Dutch West India Company sent ships with settlers to the Hudson River Valley.

The Dutch settled parts of what are now Connecticut, Delaware, New Jersey, and New York. They named this region New Netherland. They founded a seaport near the mouth of the Hudson and named it New Amsterdam.

During the 1660's, England and the Netherlands fought several wars. In 1664, a **fleet** of English warships entered the harbor at New Amsterdam. They forced the Dutch to surrender their colony of New Netherland. The English renamed the colony New York, in honor of the king's brother, the Duke of York. They renamed New Amsterdam New York City.

Ships arrive at New York Harbor in 1667. The English took over the colony of New Netherland in 1664. They renamed it New York.

The East Indies

Portuguese explorers were the first Europeans to reach the Spice Islands in Asia. In 1511, Portugal occupied the city of Melaka on the Malay Peninsula in what is now Malaysia. From this base, they controlled the Spice Islands, also known as the East Indies.

In 1602, a group of Dutch investors formed the Dutch East India Company to promote trade and colonization in Asia. Dutch warships drove the Portuguese out of Melaka in 1641 and the rest of the East Indies soon afterward. The Dutch East India Company then ruled the region. For the next 300 years, Dutch traders reaped the riches of the Spice Islands and other parts of the East Indies. In the 1940's, much of the territory they controlled became the independent nation of Indonesia.

South Africa

In the 1650's, the Dutch East India Company sent ships and colonists to southern Africa. The company started a settlement at what is now Cape Town, South Africa, near the Cape of Good Hope. The location was ideal to resupply ships on the **route** around Africa to India and other parts of Asia.

The Dutch settlers came to be known as the Boers. Today they make up part of the population of South Africa. The Boers have their own language, called Afrikaans. It grew out of the Dutch spoken by the original settlers.

The Dutch East India Company headquarters in Amsterdam in the 1600's included warehouses for storing incoming and outgoing goods and its own yard for building ships. The company helped establish Dutch rule in what is now Indonesia.

The Spice Islands are a group of Indonesian islands lying near the equator. They are now known as Maluku or the Moluccas. It was spices from these islands that first attracted European traders to the Indonesian region.

The North American Colonies

By the mid-1700's, there were 13 English colonies strung along the east coast of North America. These colonies were home to well over 1 million people.

Trade and growth

Over time, the American colonies became prosperous. Trade between the colonies and England helped cities grow. In 1775, the largest city in the American colonies was Philadelphia, with over 20,000 people. On the other side of the ocean, the busy trade with the colonies boosted the growth of cities, too. Bristol, a seaport in southwestern England, had a population of about 100,000 in 1760. London's population at about the same time was 750,000.

Ships continually sailed back and forth between England and the colonies. However, ocean travel in sailing ships of the 1700's was often unpleasant and dangerous. It was not uncommon for ships to be lost at sea in storms.

Native Americans trade furs with colonists aboard a European ship.

The Thirteen Colonies and the dates of their first permanent settlements

Virginia	1607	Delaware	1638
Massachusetts	1620	Pennsylvania	1643
New Hampshire	1623	North Carolina	c. 1653
New York	1624	New Jersey	1660
Connecticut	1633	South Carolina	1670
Maryland	1634	Georgia	1733
Rhode Island	1636		

New France

France's colony of New France was prosperous, too. In New France, most settlements were along the St. Lawrence River in what is now the Canadian province of Quebec. In 1754, this region had a European population of just under 60,000. Quebec, the colony's largest city, had a population of about 8,000.

Like the British colonies farther south, New France relied heavily on ocean shipping. Ships allowed trade between France and its colonies. They also made it possible for the French king to rule his colony effectively.

The fur trade was the chief **economic** activity in New France. Many colonists lived along the frontiers and made their living trading with Indians for furs. They were called *coureurs de bois* (runners in the woods) or *voyageurs* (voyagers). These fur traders traveled by land or on rivers and lakes in canoes similar to those made by Indians of northeastern North America.

The end of New France

In 1759, British forces conquered the city of Quebec. In 1763, Britain signed a peace treaty with France. In that treaty, France gave up all of its lands in present-day Canada to Britain.

The French fur trade in North America flourished between 1500 and 1763.

British forces land on the banks of Quebec in 1763.

Exploring the Pacific

Over a period of hundreds of years, explorers gradually mapped the vast Pacific Ocean and its many islands.

In 1520 and 1521, Ferdinand Magellan became the first European explorer to cross the Pacific Ocean. About 50 years later, another European explorer, England's Sir Francis Drake, repeated the feat. Drake sailed from England in 1577 and returned in 1580. He sailed up the western coast of the Americas in Pacific waters. He then crossed the Pacific Ocean from the coast of what is now Oregon to the Philippine Islands.

China and Japan

Portuguese explorers were the first Europeans to sail all the way to China and Japan. They sailed there from their **forts** on the Spice Islands. In 1557, the Portuguese set up a permanent colony in Macau (sometimes spelled Macao). Macau is on the south coast of China near the present-day city of Hong Kong.

The Portuguese also landed in Japan. They sent missionaries to convert the Japanese to the Catholic religion. The missionaries also helped Portuguese traders sell European goods to the Japanese.

In the early 1600's, Japan expelled most foreigners. For more than 200 years, Japan did not open its door again to outsiders.

In the 1850's, the United States naval officer Matthew C. Perry opened Japan to Western trade and diplomacy.

The Pacific Islands are thousands of islands scattered across the Pacific Ocean. They include the Hawaiian Islands and Tahiti.

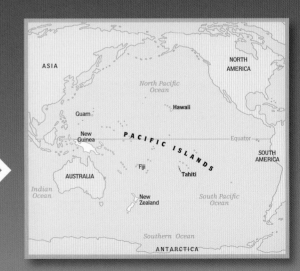

Exploring the Pacific Islands

Despite Magellan's and Drake's world voyages, most explorers and traders focused their attentions on the new lands of the Americas or on the rich and productive lands of Asia. By the 1700's, however, people became more curious about the immense Pacific Ocean and islands it might contain.

Between 1766 and 1769, a French scientist and explorer, Louis-Antoine Bougainville, explored the Pacific. In 1768, Bougainville landed on the small **tropical** island of Tahiti. Tahiti lies in the open Pacific about 3,000 miles (4,800 kilometers) south of Hawaii. Soon after, the English sea captain Samuel Wallis explored Tahiti and other Pacific Islands.

James Cook's Pacific voyages

James Cook, a British naval captain, made three Pacific voyages between 1768 and 1779. Cook became the first European to go ashore in New Zealand. He was the first European to report having visited the Hawaiian Islands. Cook landed there in 1778. He charted and mapped a number of other Pacific Islands. Among them are Easter Island, the Marquesas Islands, the Tuamotu Islands, New Caledonia, Tonga, New Hebrides (now Vanuatu), the Cook Islands, and Tahiti.

James Cook explored many islands in the Pacific Ocean. He landed on the Hawaiian Islands in 1778.

James Cook was killed in Hawaii in a dispute between his crew and the natives in 1779.

Exploring Australia and New Zealand

For a long time, European explorers did not know that the land we now know as Australia was a huge continent. In time, explorers mapped Australia and its neighbor, New Zealand.

In 1840, Maori leaders of New Zealand and the British signed the Treaty of Waitangi. The treaty is considered New Zealand's founding document.

As Europeans explored Southeast Asia and Pacific lands, they came to realize that an unknown land lay to the south and east. In the 1640's, a Dutch sea captain named Abel Tasman sailed south from the Dutch East Indies to explore this mysterious land. Tasman discovered the island of Tasmania, which was named for him. But even though he sailed completely around Australia, he never sighted it.

Voyages to Australia

In 1770, British naval captain James Cook became the first European to travel along the east coast of Australia. He named it New South Wales. Cook mapped much of the east coast of Australia. He was certain that it was part of an enormous land mass.

Within 20 years, the first groups of British settlers came to Australia. They encountered native peoples who came to be known as Aborigines *(AB uh RIHJ uh neez)*. Scientists believe that the Australian Aborigines came to the continent by boat from Southeast Asia at least 50,000 years ago.

Australian Aborigines are the first people of Australia. Many Aboriginal people have preserved the traditions and way of life of their ancestors.

Voyages to New Zealand

In 1642, Abel Tasman visited New Zealand. Tasman's visit to New Zealand was part of a greater voyage of exploration in which he also visited the island of Tasmania off the south coast of Australia. Tasman anchored his ship in a bay in New Zealand but did not set foot on land.

In 1768, Captain James Cook visited New Zealand and mapped its coasts. Cook made two additional visits to New Zealand between 1772 and 1778. He claimed New Zealand for Britain. The first British settlers began arriving in the early 1800's.

New Zealand, like Australia, had long-settled inhabitants. These were a Polynesian people whose descendants came to be called the Maori *(MOW ree)*. (The Polynesians came originally from Southeast Asia. They spread out among the many islands in the Pacific.) No one knows for sure when the Polynesians first arrived in New Zealand. Some scientists believe that it was around A.D. 1200.

Words, Words, Words

The word *Aborigines* comes from the Latin phrase *ab origine*, which means *from the beginning*. A different form of the word can be used as an adjective, or describing word: *Aboriginal*. Both the noun and the adjective are capitalized when one is writing about Australian Aborigines.

British ships arrive in Sydney Cove on January 26, 1788. The **fleet** established the first permanent European settlement in Australia.

◄ Abel Tasman's voyage to Tasmania and New Zealand. During his 1642–1643 voyage—marked by a green line—Tasman traveled around Australia, but he did not sight the mainland. On a second voyage in 1644—marked by a red line—Tasman explored the northern coast of Australia.

India
ASIA
AFRICA
Philippines
Pacific Ocean
Equator
Equator
Batavia (Jakarta)
1644
New Guinea
1643
1642
Java
Solomon Islands
Madagascar
Timor Sea
Cape York Peninsula
Fiji
Mauritius
1644
Gulf of Carpentaria
Tonga
Tropic of Capricorn
New Holland
1643
Indian Ocean
Tasman Sea
Murderers' Bay
0   1,000 Miles
1642
Staten Land
0   1,000 Kilometers
1642
Van Diemen's Land

Exploring Alaska and the Pacific Northwest

During the 1700's, Europeans gradually explored Alaska and the Pacific coastline of what is now the Canadian province of British Columbia. Some explorers also visited parts of what are now the U.S. states of Washington and Oregon.

By the early 1700's, explorers had visited much of North America. However, the northwestern part of the continent remained unexplored and unknown. Some explorers turned their attention to these lands.

Russian explorers

During the 1600's, Russians explored Siberia, a huge region in northwestern Asia, and claimed it for their czar (ruler). As they expanded their huge nation eastward all the way to the North Pacific Ocean, they began to wonder what was beyond it.

In 1728, Vitus Bering *(VEE tus BAIR ihng or BEER ihng),* a Danish sea captain hired by the Russian czar, explored the strait between Siberia and Alaska. It is now called the Bering Strait, in honor of him. However, because of dense fog, Bering did not see Alaska.

Then in 1741, Bering led another **expedition** into the Bering Strait. This time, the explorer found the Alaska coast and claimed the land for Russia.

About 40 years later, in 1784, the Russians set up a colony on Kodiak Island. The island lies about 35 miles (56 kilometers) off the southern coast of Alaska.

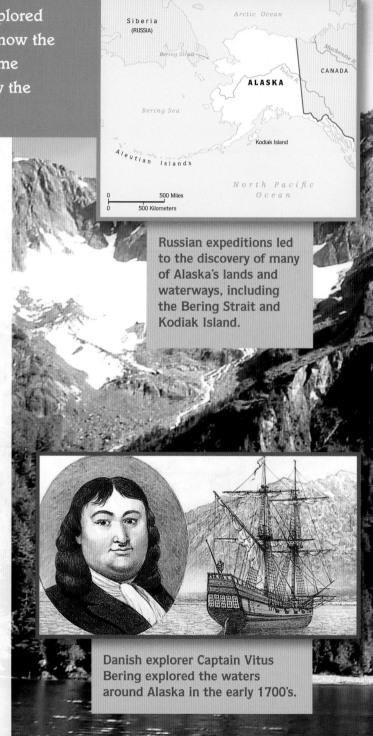

Russian expeditions led to the discovery of many of Alaska's lands and waterways, including the Bering Strait and Kodiak Island.

Danish explorer Captain Vitus Bering explored the waters around Alaska in the early 1700's.

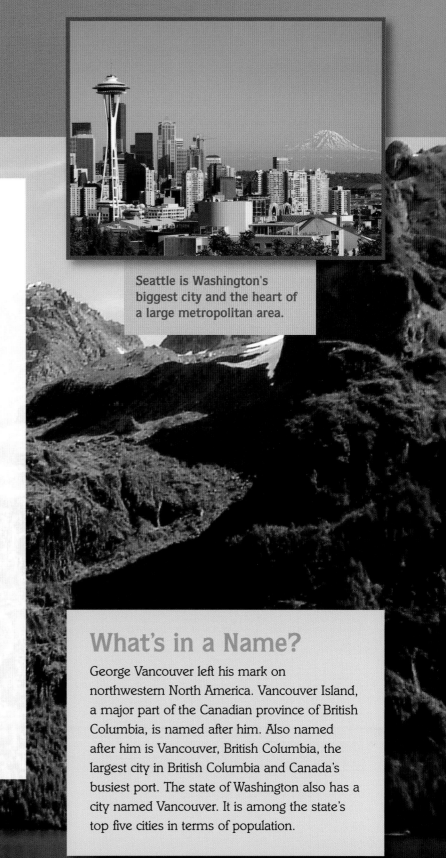

George Vancouver

A number of talented English sailors received valuable training on the expeditions of Captain Cook. One of them was George Vancouver.

In 1791, the British government ordered Vancouver to lead a **fleet** of British ships to the northwest Pacific coast of North America. Vancouver was to meet with a Spanish official to solve a dispute between Spain and Britain over a trading post in the region.

Vancouver followed Pacific Ocean **routes** established by Captain Cook. In April 1792, he sailed through the Strait of Juan de Fuca between Victoria Island and what is now the state of Washington. Vancouver then entered Puget Sound. The explorer made a landing north of what is now the city of Seattle and claimed the land for Britain. Vancouver named many natural features in the region, including Puget Sound and Mt. Rainier.

Vancouver made detailed charts and maps of the Puget Sound region. These were extremely useful to later explorers and settlers.

Seattle is Washington's biggest city and the heart of a large metropolitan area.

What's in a Name?

George Vancouver left his mark on northwestern North America. Vancouver Island, a major part of the Canadian province of British Columbia, is named after him. Also named after him is Vancouver, British Columbia, the largest city in British Columbia and Canada's busiest port. The state of Washington also has a city named Vancouver. It is among the state's top five cities in terms of population.

The British Empire Dominates Trade

By the end of the 1700's, the British Empire was spread across the globe. Great Britain and its colonies dominated world trade.

As the Age of Exploration began around 1500, powerful European nations began to expand overseas and form **empires.** Building an empire required a strong navy, wealth to invest in colonization, and a strong government in the home country. The first world empires were the Spanish and Portuguese empires. But in time, England and France built world empires, too.

England comes out on top

As time went on, Spain and Portugal declined, though they kept their empires. For a time, England and France competed for colonies and fought one war after another. But by the end of the 1700's, England's empire eclipsed that of France. The biggest blow to France was the loss of its colony of New France to England (now part of the United Kingdom) in 1763.

The British Empire experienced a setback in 1783, when its North American colonies achieved independence as the United States. However, the United Kingdom recovered. It went on to develop valuable colonies in India, Africa, Southeast Asia, and other places.

▲ During the 1800's, the British colony of Hong Kong became one of Asia's most important trade and commercial centers.

What's in a Name?

When we speak of the nation on the southern part of the island of Great Britain, we often speak of "England." However, in 1707, England and Scotland formed a union called the United Kingdom. So for dates after 1707, it is usually more accurate to speak of "the United Kingdom" rather than "England." Also for these later dates, it is usually clearer to use the term *British* rather than *English*.

The sun never sets ...

At the height of the British Empire, in the 1800's and early 1900's, people often said, "The sun never sets on the British Empire." Its colonies were spread all around the globe.

Some of the richest British colonies were in Asia. These included the huge country of India; Hong Kong, just off the southern coast of China; and Singapore, a key port in Southeast Asia.

Because of this far-flung empire, good transportation by sea was extremely important to the British. The United Kingdom became a leader in shipbuilding and in developing new technology for ships.

By the late 1800's, most ships used in international trade were steamships powered by coal. Using these ships on long voyages required occasional stops at coaling stations. (A coaling station is a port where steamships can take on coal as fuel.) Some British colonies were started mainly as coaling stations. One such colony was the island of Mauritius (maw RIHSH uhs) off the east coast of Africa.

The Chronometer

Since the early days of the Age of Exploration, sea captains possessed tools that allowed them to figure out their **latitude.** However, they could only guess at longitude. (*Latitude* is how far north or south one is; *longitude* is how far east or west.)

To determine latitude, ship captains needed an accurate clock. However, the clock of the time had a pendulum (a weighted rod that swings back and forth). The clock's pendulum kept good time on land but not on a choppy sea.

In 1714, the British government offered a cash prize to anyone who could build an accurate chronometer (timepiece) for use at sea. In the 1730's, John Harrison made such a chronometer— but it took him a lifetime to collect his prize.

Territories of the British Empire during colonial times, through the 1920's, and its territories today.

The Age of Imperialism

In the 1800's and early 1900's, European countries controlled colonies throughout most of the world. This era is often called the Age of Imperialism. Imperialism describes when one country rules over other countries and colonies.

The British brought to their territories new customs and ways of life. During their rule in India, the British converted large areas of land for tea production. India remains one of the largest producers of tea leaves.

When Columbus stepped onto San Salvador Island in October 1492, he could not have foreseen the future. However, in hindsight, it does not seem surprising that powerful European countries would, in time, colonize much of the world. And that is exactly what happened.

European colonies

By 1900, European countries had planted colonies throughout the world. Many countries that were still technically free were controlled by European nations or companies. Belgium, France, the Netherlands, Portugal, Spain, and the United Kingdom held colonies across the globe.

Some of these countries, as well as Russia and Japan, also controlled much of China. Although China had been a powerful nation with a high civilization (organized society), by 1850 it was almost powerless against the demands of European powers. European governments and companies plundered (stole from) much of China.

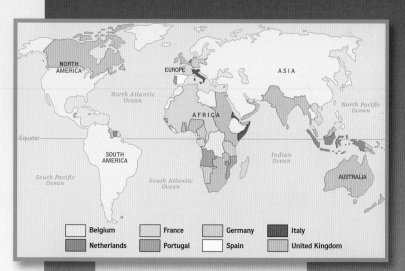

European colonial **empires** had spread over much of the world by the late 1800's. The largest empire belonged to the United Kingdom, whose possessions included Australia, Canada, India, and parts of Africa.

Words, Words, Words

During the Age of Imperialism, the colonizing nations were strongly affected by the cultures of their colonies. Many words from languages of colonized people entered European languages. These words, for example, have entered the English language:

- banana (from a language of West Africa)
- boomerang (from a language of the Australian Aborigines)
- chimpanzee (from a language of West Africa)
- cot (from Hindi, a language of India)
- jungle (from Hindi, a language of India)
- shampoo (from Hindi, a language of India)
- tea (from Mandarin, a language of China)

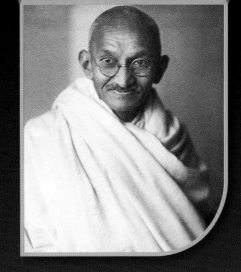

Mohandas K. Gandhi helped win independence for India from the United Kingdom. He preached nonviolence in his long campaign for freedom and social reform.

The British controlled gold and diamond mines in South Africa during the height of their power.

Dwindling power

The control that the European colonial powers exercised across the globe did not last forever. Several things happened.

To begin with, the European nations fought among themselves in two terrible world wars: World War I (1914–1918) and World War II (1939–1945). These wars weakened European control over their colonies.

Perhaps more importantly, people in countries colonized by Europe began to work hard for independence. In 1947, for example, a visionary Indian leader, Mohandas Gandhi, and a practical politician, Jawaharlal Nehru, led India to independence from the United Kingdom. African peoples worked for independence, too. Most colonized African nations won their independence by the 1960's and 1970's.

Many people saw an event that took place in 1997 as marking the end of European imperialism. In that year, the United Kingdom turned over its rich Hong Kong colony to the People's Republic of China. Today, China is the second-largest **economy** in the world.

Glossary

economy (n.); economic (adj.) a system of managing the production, distribution, and consumption of goods and services; having to do with the management of the income, supplies, and expenses of a household, community, government, or other group or organization.

emperor a person who is the ruler of an empire.

empire a group of nations or states under one ruler or government, with one country having some measure of control over the rest.

expedition a journey made for some special purpose.

fleet a group of warships, naval aircraft, personnel, and bases under one command.

fort a strong building or place that can be defended against an enemy; fortified place.

latitude distance north or south of the equator, measured in degrees.

Middle Ages the period in European history between ancient and modern times, from about the A.D. 400's through the 1400's.

Muslim a follower of Muhammad; believer in Islam, the religion founded by him.

navigate (v.); navigation (n.) to sail, manage, or steer (a ship, aircraft, or rocket) on a course or to a destination; the act of navigating.

navigator a person who sails the seas.

New World another name for the Western Hemisphere, which includes the continents of North America and South America.

Roman Empire the empire of ancient Rome that lasted from 27 B.C., when it was established by Augustus, to A.D. 395, when it was divided into the Eastern Roman Empire, or Byzantine Empire (A.D. 395-1453), and the Western Roman Empire (A.D. 395-476).

route a way to go; path.

tropical having to do with the tropics—the area of Earth lying just to the north and south of the equator.

Books

Around the World in a Hundred Years: From Henry the Navigator to Magellan by Jean Fritz and Anthony Bacon Venti (Putnam's, 1994)

Braving the North Atlantic: The Vikings, the Cabots, and Jacques Cartier Voyage to America by Delno C. West and Jean M. West (Atheneum Books for Young Readers,1996)

Da Gama: Vasco Da Gama Sails Around the Cape of Good Hope by Robin S. Doak (Compass Point Books, 2002)

Explorers of the Ancient World by Anthony Brierley (Peter Bedrick Books, 1995)

Marco Polo and the Wonders of the East by Hal Marcovitz (Chelsea House Publishers, 2000)

The Remarkable Voyages of Captain Cook by Rhoda Blumberg (Maxwell Macmillan International, 1991)

The Slave Trade and the Middle Passage by S. Pearl Sharp and Virginia Schomp (Marshall Cavendish Benchmark, 2007)

Who Was First? Discovering the Americas by Russell Freedman (Clarion Books, 2007)

Websites

The Age of Exploration
http://www.marinersmuseum.org/education/age-exploration

The Mariners' Museum provides this online exhibition featuring biographies, timelines, and activities.

The Conquistadors
http://www.pbs.org/opb/conquistadors/home.htm

Spanish conquistadors began to arrive in North and South America in the 1400's and 1500's. Learn about what they found there on this interactive educational site.

Empire of the Bay
http://www.pbs.org/empireofthebay/home.html

Look back at the explorers and traders who ventured into North America seeking fortune, fur, and a path to the East.

Famous People: Christopher Columbus
http://www.bbc.co.uk/schools/famouspeople/standard/columbus/index.shtml#focus

Click through a slide show to learn about Columbus's life and journeys on this educational site from the BBC.

Jump Back in Time: Colonial America
http://www.americaslibrary.gov/jb/colonial/jb_colonial_subj.html

This website from the Library of Congress features stories about the land that would eventually become the United States, from its discovery to its settlement and beyond.

My Journey on the Silk Road
http://www.amnh.org/exhibitions/silkroad/journey.php

Videos, images, and sounds bring Marco Polo's journey to life on this website from the American Museum of Natural History.

The Navigators
http://www.abc.net.au/navigators/

Learn about the ships, sailors, and scientists who first sailed to the uncharted lands of Australia.

Primary History: The Vikings
http://www.bbc.co.uk/schools/primaryhistory/vikings/

Timelines, maps, and pictures tell the stories of the Vikings, both at home and abroad.

Renaissance: Exploration and Trade
http://www.learner.org/interactives/renaissance/exploration.html

Learn about navigation, explore the New World, and try out the life of a spice trader at this educational site.

Index